HOW TO BECOME YOUR HUSBAND'S BEST FRIEND

Gary Smalley

PYRANEE
BOOKS

Zondervan Publishing House
Grand Rapids, Michigan

How to Become Your Husband's Best Friend

This is a Pyranee Book
Published by the Zondervan Publishing House
1415 Lake Drive, S.E., Grand Rapids, Michigan 49506

This book is excerpted from *For Better or For Best* copyright ©
1979 by Gary T. Smalley; revised edition copyright © 1982 by
The Zondervan Corporation.

Library of Congress Cataloging in Publication Data

Smalley, Gary.
    How to become your husband's best friend.

    Excerpted from For better or for best.
    "Pyranee Books."
    1. Marriage. 2. Interpersonal relations. I. Title.
HQ734.S6832   1985   646.7'8   85-14209
ISBN 0-310-44992-8

Unless otherwise indicated, the Scripture text used is the *New
American Standard Bible*, copyright © 1960, 1962, 1963, 1968,
1971, 1972 by the Lockman Foundation, La Habra, California.

Printed in the United States of America

86   87   88   89   90 / 10   9   8   7

Contents

THE BEST IN WHOLESOME READING
DISTRIBUTED BY
CHOICE BOOKS
P.O. BOX 243, VIENNA, VA. 22180
WE WELCOME YOUR RESPONSE

1

How to Become Your Husband's Best Friend

"It is not good for a man to be alone; I will make him a helper suitable for him."
—*Genesis 2:18*

The most important objective of this book is to help you become your husband's best friend. A best friend is someone with whom you share intimately, someone with whom you love to spend time. Maybe that doesn't describe your husband's feelings for you at present—or your feelings for him. But don't give up hope. We will discuss some ways you *can* become his closest companion.

Share Common Experiences Together

Within a period of three years, I interviewed more than thirty families who were very satisfied with their inner-family relationships. Theirs was not a superficial satisfaction, but a deep love and fulfillment. The families came from diverse geographical and social settings, and their economic bases ranged from very modest to very wealthy. But all the families had two things in common, one of which was a concern for togetherness. In each case, the husband and wife tried not to schedule independent activities that would take them away from each other or from their children on a consistent basis. They also avoided activities that would not contribute to the well-being of the total family.

Careful planning was an essential key in these homes. Though a certain degree of flexibility was present for the pursuit of individual interests, each family member worked to create a mutually supportive unit. The family, it seemed, became a "person" in itself, nourishing itself and protecting its best interests. Typically, the husband and wife spent some time in joint activities, but more time in activities including their children. When one of the family members participated in an individual activity, the others made an effort to support him or her. (For example, the whole family would turn out for a Little League ball game.)

The other striking factor common to all these happy families was their love for *camping*. My wife and I had never been inclined toward campfires and army cots, but when I discovered that all thirty "ideal" families were campers, we decided to give it a try.

I borrowed a "pop-up camper" and we made plans to camp our way from Chicago to Florida. The first night on the road, we arrived in Kentucky. It was a beautiful night, and I thought, *I can really see why this draws families together.* We talked around the campfire, sang songs, and roasted hot dogs. By nine o'clock we were pleasantly tired and tucked in bed. A romantic bit of lightning flashed in the distance followed by a gentle roll of thunder. Then it happened! That gentle thunder became a deafening boom that seemed to hover over our camper. Terror seized my little troop. Rain beat against our camper so hard that it forced its way in and soaked our pillows.

Norma and I were frozen in terror when she squeaked, "Do you think the camper will blow over?"

"Not a chance," I said. *But it might blow up,* I thought to myself.

Who would consider camping after a horror

7

story like that? We did. In fact, we've endured far worse at times. It seems some of our worst tragedies and arguments happen on camping trips. And that's precisely why we've become avid campers. So many things can go wrong that a family is *forced* to unite just to make it through the tough parts of the trip. The good side of camping enables a couple and their children to share the beautiful sights and sounds of God's creation. For years afterward, they can reflect on the tragic and happy experiences they struggled through together. The feeling of oneness lingers *long* after the camping trip is over.

Your first attempt at scheduling family activities may be difficult due to overcommitment. If your husband or family is already worn out with too many activities, they won't be exuberant over your new ideas. You may even be too tired to consider them yourself. But you can *make* time for them by learning to use the simple word "no." When you are asked to commit yourself to an activity that you know would not benefit your family in the long run, simply say no. Or tell them you need to discuss it with your husband. If necessary, let him step in and act as a shield by saying no.

Not all individual activities are nonproductive or harmful to family life. Your love for antiques and your son's love for caterpillars make for a healthy balance. There is no reason to cut out or infringe upon all individual interests. Flexibility will allow togetherness and individuality.

However, one family member should not expect another to participate in distasteful or offensive activities. And no family member should attempt to be another's conscience. I don't believe you should force yourself to violate your own conscience just to be together as a family. (Not participating in distasteful activities is an important part of Romans 14.) Neither should you condemn those in your family for any of their activities. If a certain family function is distasteful, simply share in a gentle, noncondemning way that you would rather not participate. I have found that when a wife stands firm on her personal convictions in a nonjudgmental manner, it only adds to her family's respect for her.

Attack and Conquer Tragedies As a Couple Not As Individuals

Lasting friendships are built in foxholes. Nothing binds two people together faster than a common struggle against the enemy. Virtually any crisis can draw you and your husband closer, whether it be a stopped-up sink or your unwed daughter's pregnancy. No one hunts for tragedy, but if it strikes at your door, you can strengthen your marriage by dealing with it as a team.

One of America's great preachers tells how a tremendous sorrow united his family. He and his wife faced the "typical" marriage problems and their teenagers were going through the "typical" years of rebellion. Their family life was pleasant but not intimate. One day, to everyone's amazement, his wife came home and announced she was pregnant. No one was unusually excited; the last thing they felt they needed was another mouth to feed and keep quiet.

Soon after the baby was born, things changed. He became the apple of everyone's eye. His sweet, gentle spirit was apparent from the day he came home from the hospital. The children were so in love with him they argued over who would get to baby-sit with him. When the baby was only a year old, he became very ill and had to be rushed to the hospital. The whole family waited anxiously for the doctor's report. That sweet little boy had leukemia. For three days and nights the family waited together in a single room, watching over their baby, praying and hoping he would live. On the third day he died. Overwhelmed with grief, they went home to start a new life without him. Never again would they take one another for granted. Their mutual love and commitment would remain strong. Without a doubt, the death of their baby was the greatest tragedy any of them had ever experienced, but out of it came a tremendous love, intimacy, and appreciation for each family member.

Make Important Decisions Together

It was the Fourth of July, and Norma and I were getting ready for a picnic when we broke into a heated argument. After a few minutes, things had only gotten worse. We could see we were going to be late for the picnic, so we postponed the argument till later.

I was fed up with our history of arguments. It seemed we couldn't stay out of a fight for a day. I asked Norma, "Would you be willing to try a new approach for a few weeks?" She agreed.

What we agreed upon that day has had a powerful impact on our marriage. It has forced us to communicate on deeper levels than I ever thought existed, helping us to gain an understanding of our individual viewpoints. It has forced us to look beneath surface opinions and discover the very root of our own thinking. When we disagree about a situation, our commitment to this principle helps us verbalize our feelings until we understand each other. Six years have passed since we made that commitment, and it continues to work far beyond our expectations. (It's been keeping us out of arguments ever since!)

On that Fourth of July *we agreed never to make final decisions on matters that affected both of us unless we both agreed.* If we don't arrive at unity before the bus gets here, we don't get on it. We've relied on this principle in all sorts of situations. Both of us assume responsibility for sharing our feelings honestly because we know we can't go anywhere until we're in agreement.

One man told me he would have saved more than thirty thousand dollars in the stock market if he had put this principle into action six months earlier. I'm always glad to find men who are willing to admit the value of their wives' counsel. After all, no one knows a man better than his "best friend."

Develop a Sense of Humor

Class reunions always bring out the funny memories of former days. Here in this corner Jack is breaking up the group clustered around him with his old sophomore jokes. Over there by the punch bowl Janet is laughing uncontrollably as she's reminded of that practical joke on her first double-date. It seems we all did more laughing in our premarital days.

You probably weren't somber and sad when your husband married you. So, if you want to be his best friend now, you may need to add a little humor to your relationship. No need to buy a clown suit. Just look for ways to tickle his funny bone. Clip those comics or cartoons that strike you as funny and save them for his enjoyment during lighthearted times. Be willing to loosen up and laugh heartily when he tells a good joke. There are countless ways to add humor to your marriage. Be willing to set aside the serious quest for romance at times to enjoy just having fun together as friends.

Understand Your Own Personality Traits and Your Husband's

We didn't develop all our personality traits. Many of them were inborn. There are four basic temperaments that affect our personalities and all of us *tend* toward one of those temperaments. According to Tim LaHaye, these four personality types can be labeled the talker, the leader, the legalist, and the unmotivated. If you don't understand your personality type and the way it interacts with your husband's, you are likely to suffer unnecessary pain and misunderstanding. Each personality type has its strengths and weaknesses. When you better understand the strengths and weaknesses of your husband's personality, you can work in harmony with him to compensate for his weakness. If you don't understand his personality type, you may react to his weaknesses whenever they clash with yours.

There is so much material on the subject of personality types that to go into detail would require another book. However, I have attempted to give a brief description of each personality type, some of its strengths, and some of its weaknesses.

Take this simple test to determine your own personality type and your husband's type. (You each might be a combination of two types.) Check the appropriate boxes with an X for your husband and an O for you. The point of the test is to show that each of us has a unique

The Outgoing Types (Extrovert)		The Shy Types (Introvert)	
I The Talker	II The Leader	III The Legalist	IV The Unmotivated
☐ forward looking	☐ cold—unsympathetic	☐ gifted	☐ calm & quiet
☐ inventive	☐ determined & strong-willed	☐ moody	☐ casual
☐ undisciplined	☐ insensitive & inconsiderate	☐ analytical	☐ easygoing
☐ charming	☐ independent	☐ negative	☐ idle
☐ weak-willed	☐ hostile—angry	☐ perfectionist	☐ likeable
☐ restless	☐ productive	☐ critical	☐ spectator
☐ warm	☐ cruel—sarcastic	☐ conscientious	☐ diplomatic
☐ friendly	☐ decisive	☐ rigid & legalist	☐ selfish
☐ disorganized	☐ unforgiving	☐ loyal	☐ stingy
☐ responsive	☐ self-sufficient	☐ self-centered	☐ dependable
☐ unproductive	☐ visionary	☐ aesthetic	☐ stubborn
☐ talkative	☐ domineering	☐ touchy	☐ conservative
☐ undependable	☐ optimistic	☐ idealistic	☐ self-protective
☐ enthusiastic	☐ opinionated & prejudiced	☐ revengeful	☐ practical
☐ obnoxious—loud	☐ courageous	☐ sensitive	☐ indecisive
☐ carefree	☐ proud	☐ persecution-prone	☐ reluctant leader
☐ egocentric	☐ self-confident	☐ self-sacrificing	☐ fearful
☐ compassionate	☐ crafty	☐ unsociable	☐ dry humor
☐ exaggerates	☐ leader	☐ self-disciplined	
☐ generous		☐ theoretical & impractical	
☐ fearful & insecure			

personality type and that we *tend* to marry opposites (those who complement us).

Becoming best friends is not an automatic process just because you live together. You have to learn to compensate when you are confronted daily with the faults and weaknesses of your mate. Your "best friend" relationship with him will require perseverance, patience, understanding, genuine love, and the other qualities we discussed throughout this book. As you put into practice the five suggestions we discussed in this chapter, I am confident your friendship will deepen.

For Personal Reflection

List the specific ways you have been a helper or completer to your husband (Genesis 2:18).

List additional ways you could help or complete his life.

2

How to Gain Your Husband's Comfort Instead of Criticism

"To sum up,
let all be harmonious,
sympathetic, brotherly,
kindhearted, and humble
in spirit;
not returning
evil for evil,
or insult for insult,
but giving a blessing."

—*1 Peter 3:8–9*

It was the dead of winter, and Lois felt as if she had been cooped up in the house for weeks. She had been invited to a women's luncheon so she jumped at the chance to get out of the house. She got in her car, turned the key, and to her dismay found that the battery was dead. Realizing her plans were ruined, she rummaged through her purse for the house keys.

Suddenly she remembered she had left the keys inside the house. It was definitely "one of those days" ... she couldn't go to the luncheon, she couldn't get into the house, her neighbors weren't home, and there wasn't a phone nearby. Her only choice was to trudge to a phone in the bitter weather. On the way, a high school student recognized her and offered her a ride. She decided to go to her husband's office instead. Discouraged and depressed, she needed her husband's comfort.

Enter husband—irritated and angry. He just couldn't believe she had locked herself out of the house. And to top it all off, she had the gall to embarrass him by coming to his office during work hours. Just so it wouldn't happen again, he let the harsh words fly. Of course, his words produced nothing but more frustration and hurt feelings in Lois.

Why do men find it much easier to lecture their wives than to comfort them? If you could climb into a man's mind, you would see that when he is confused or hurt he seeks a *logical explanation* for his feelings. Once he has made a clear analysis of the problem, he usually feels relieved. It is only "logical," then, that he respond to your problems in the same way. In essence, he thinks he can "talk you out of it."

But if your relationship with your husband is to be strengthened, it's vitally important that he learn when and how to comfort you. You shouldn't feel guilty about your need for someone to "lean on." That need is not a sign of weakness, as some would have you believe. It's simply a part of our human nature. We all need to lean at times.

Get Excited Over His Attempts to Comfort You

The first step in motivating your husband to comfort you is to respond in a big way each time he does the slightest thing to comfort you. This is called *positive reinforcement*. It demonstrates how much you appreciate his understanding. I'm not telling you to try out for cheerleader each time he comforts you. Just remember to do something special for him— maybe a day, even a week later. Perhaps a special meal, a romantic night in the bedroom, or an unexpected love note in his lunch box or wallet. If there was anything you particularly liked about the way he comforted you, call attention to it. Regardless of what you do to show your appreciation, be sure he sees the link between your gratefulness and his act of comfort. Incidentally, he needs to learn how to comfort you as much as you need to receive it. He needs it for his own personal well-being and joy (John 15:11; Col. 3:12–15).

It's extremely important that you never ridicule or belittle any of your husband's attempts to comfort you. Even when his attempts are inadequate, rather than calling attention to his failure, praise him for anything positive in his actions. (Even the attempt itself is a move in the right direction!) Never try to gain his comfort by criticizing him for not comforting you.

Imagine for a moment that your son has just been taken to the hospital. You need someone to lean on emotionally. The anxiety is almost more than you can bear, but your husband just stands there. You're thinking inside *Why don't you just hold me and reassure me?* So you blurt out, "Don't just stand there. Come here and hold me." Now you've called attention to his inadequacy, compounding the anxiety and concern he feels for your son. Unfortunately, his natural response is to resist all the more.

People always respond more favorably to positive reinforcement than to negatives such as criticism or ridicule. In building your relationship, it's of utmost importance that you praise him for his attempts to be a comfort to you. But that's just the first step in motivating him to offer his emotional support.

Teach Your Husband How to Comfort by Being His Example

The second step concerns the principle of reaping and sowing. One of the most effective ways to teach your husband how to comfort you is to discover how he likes to be treated when he's down. Teach by example. When you sense that he is fearful or uncertain, ask him to tell you how he feels. Tell him you understand. If he reacts to you, saying something like, "Don't treat me like a little kid," then try another approach. Perhaps he feels unmanly or childish in your comforting arms. In that case, you can comfort him with your words and facial expressions. He won't resist when you learn to comfort him the way he needs to be comforted.

To some men, emotional support means taking their side in a conflict. For example, when John was in college, his fiancée broke their engagement and decided to marry one of his best friends. John's only consolation came when his roommate, Ted, responded with deep empathy: "John, I don't know what's wrong, but I know you're hurting. If you want

21

to talk about it, or if there's anything I can do, just say so. If you don't want to talk about it and you want to be left alone, I'll just wait in the living room until you feel a little better."

John, touched by his roommate's concern, revealed that his fiancée was marrying a friend. "I just need some time to be alone," he said.

When Ted walked into the other room, John overhead him say to his girl friend, "Your best friend Sue just went and got engaged to another guy. How do you like that?"

That was just the type of comfort John needed. His roommate really understood how he was feeling!

Try to detect the most meaningful ways to comfort your husband in each situation.

Tell Him Gently How You Desire to Be Comforted

The third step is to teach him how you, as a woman, need to be comforted. It's important to remember that his natural inclination may be to solve your problems "logically" so that they don't arise again. Much of this is covered in the book *If Only He Knew**. Chances are you'll

---

*Gary Smalley with Steve Scott, *If Only He Knew* (Grand Rapids: Zondervan, 1982).

still have to be his main teacher. After all, you're the one he is learning to comfort.

There was a woman who received a lecture virtually every time she needed comfort. She had to remind her husband four or five times, "Don't try to tell me why it happened. Just hold me." He finally got the message. Had she not persisted, he never would have learned how to comfort her. (One encouraging point: they had been married nine years before she tried to teach him how to comfort her, but it only took a few weeks for him to catch on.)

One woman who had left her husband said, "I just can't stand the thought of going back into that situation. He offends me in so many ways, and then he never comforts me when I need it. I just can't go back." I asked her if she would be willing to teach her husband how to comfort her. She gave me a funny look and asked, "What do you mean, teach him?"

"When you're in a stressful situation, or when you're discouraged, how do you want him to treat you?"

"I'd like him to put both arms around me and gently hold me. Then I'd want him to tell me that he understood or at least that he was trying to understand."

"Well, why don't you teach him that?"

"You're kidding! He'd think I was crazy. And besides, why should I have to teach him? He should do it on his own. I'd feel stupid having to tell him things like that."

I changed my approach a little. "Has he ever said things to you like, 'Honey, I don't know what you want me to do when you're discouraged. Should I cry, or kiss you, or . . . ?'"

Her eyes lit up and she said, "Yeah, it's amazing the number of times he's said that he didn't know what to do, or how to act, or what to say. I even remember him saying, 'You just tell me what you want me to do.' But I always thought he was being sarcastic, and I was offended because he couldn't figure it out by himself. I thought if I had to tell him it really wouldn't mean anything anyway. Do you mean some men really need to be taught the little things, like how to hold a woman tenderly?"

My answer was an obvious "yes." A lot of men avoid soft words and tender comfort because they have never been taught how to use them. Also, they simply don't understand the positive effects they will have on their wives and the sense of well-being they themselves will receive. I have found that once a man has learned why and how to comfort, he gains a real appreciation for the role it plays in the marital relationship.

During most of our marriage, my wife could never expect to receive comfort from me whenever she made an embarrassing mistake. I usually ridiculed her or got upset. But eventually she began to share with me her need for sympathy, compassion, and understanding. Just when I was starting to get the hang of it, my newly acquired knowledge was put to the royal test. I came home one Saturday to find my camper parked at an angle in the driveway—not unusual in itself. Unfortunately, a large section of the garage roof was lying next to it in the driveway. Like most men, the first thought that came to mind was money. How much would it cost to fix it all? I felt like going into the house and screaming at my wife for her carelessness.

As these thoughts raced through my mind, I recalled the many times she had told me how she needed to be treated in upsetting situations. I walked up to her, put my arm around her with a smile and choked out the words, "I'll bet you really feel bad. Let's go into the house and talk about it. I don't want you to feel bad for my sake."

Inside, I held her for a minute without

saying anything. She told me she had dreaded my reaction as much as the accident. "That's okay, honey," I said. "We'll fix it. Don't worry about it." The longer I held her and the more I comforted *her*, the better we felt.

When we walked out to survey the damage, I realized it wasn't sheared off as badly as it looked. The roof hadn't splintered; the part that fell had sheared off neatly like a puzzle piece. All that was needed were some nails and a little paint. Within a few minutes, a friend had heard about the accident and had driven into my driveway with a pickup and tools; in an hour we had it completely fixed.

When we were finished, I thought to myself, *A couple of hours ago I could have crushed my wife's spirit, strained our relationship, and made her feel like an idiot ... all over an hour's work.*

Even though I thought Norma would be the only one to gain from my understanding attitude, in the long run I actually benefited the most. The increased admiration and respect I received from her provided an even greater incentive for comforting her. If you let your husband know that you deeply admire him for his comfort, he, too, will have an increased desire to comfort you.

For Personal Reflection

Think of at least three future stressful situations that would cause you to desire comfort. Discuss these with your husband and explain exactly what you would need if any of the three situations occurred.

3

How to Deepen Your Husband's Affection for You

"He
who sows sparingly
shall also
reap sparingly;
and he
who sows bountifully
shall also
reap bountifully."

—*2 Corinthians 9:6*

Tim glanced across the breakfast table at Ruth. As he looked at her, he came to a sickening realization—"I don't feel any love for her anymore . . . why am I even married to this woman?"

Obviously, Tim's ailment couldn't be cured with two aspirin and plenty of fluids. He was suffering from the age-old problem of unrealistic expectations, thinking his mate would always be the twenty-year-old he married. But she had changed in the past eight years.

Typically, most of us expect our mates to retain their original physical and emotional attractiveness. But a funny thing happens on the way to retirement . . . we change. And if we change the things our mates once found attractive, we have to replace them with something better.

Even in the courtship phase of your relationship, his affection for you didn't "just happen." It grew in response to something he liked about you. Perhaps his feelings were stirred by your appearance, your personality, or the way you made him feel. If you have disposed of those positive qualities, his love for you may have dwindled to apathy.

During the courtship days, you probably had limited exposure to your fiancé. It was easy for each of you to put the other's needs or best interests first since you didn't have to do it twenty-four hours a day. Obviously, if your fiancé was putting your best interests first and fulfilling your needs to the neglect of his own, your heart was melting daily in response to him, and vice versa.

After marriage, things quickly changed. The

exposure was no longer limited to times when you were both "at your best." For each, your own interests began to take precedence over the other's. Under these circumstances it didn't take long for swelling affections to subside.

That's why "the other woman" is at such an advantage. She can offer the new attractions your husband assumes you have lost. She can quickly stir the deep, romantic feelings your husband longs to feel toward you. In the context of their brief encounters, both of them can temporarily subdue their self-centered natures and put the best foot forward.

What specifically can you do to increase your inward beauty that is naturally reflected through your eyes and facial expressions and definitely increases your attractiveness?

Keep a Spark Burning

There are several ways you can "keep a small spark burning" in your husband's heart for you. I know that you would love to see your husband initiate romance, but you may have to light the fire yourself for a while. Even though you begin to practice some of the following ideas, your husband may not fall head-over-heels in love with you overnight. However, his affections will change gradually. So don't be surprised if someday you wake up and he's the one kissing *you* on the cheek. Be prepared, in the meantime, for his shock, laughter, or even negative response to your romantic attempts. Just let him know that you love him and that you are trying to express your love in special ways. The ideas I suggest are by no means all encompassing. There are probably thousands of ways to bring romance into your relationship. It is hoped that mine will serve as a springboard for your own creative ways.

Plan activities that will make him feel special.

Here you can let your imagination run wild. Although the possibilities are endless, you know what types of activities would make your husband feel special. Perhaps his favorite meal by candlelight or a weekend getaway to his favorite resort. Whatever the activity, you can always enhance it by wearing his favorite perfume or a dress he really likes.

By planning special activities from time to time and adding a little variety, you will be showing him how special you think he is. He may not offer praise right away. Don't expect it. If you persist, eventually he will respond with praise and increased affection.

Occasionally be the initiator in the sexual relationship.

Men usually initiate sexual advances in marriage and do not really need preparation to be sexually aroused. A woman, on the other hand, needs to be prepared with gentle loving romance. Her responsiveness to sexual advances may even be affected by her husband's behavior over the past days and weeks. Although you understand this, your husband may not. Even though it may seem unnatural, it is important that you occasionally initiate intimacy if you wish to increase his affection for you.

If you have been belittled, crushed, criticized, or beaten down through the years, it may be extremely difficult for you to initiate sex. Many women have said that making love with their husbands without being emotionally prepared makes them feel like prostitutes. For a woman to engage freely in love-making, she has to give her whole self to her lover. When she is unable to do this because of his bad treatment or inadequate preparation, she feels as if he is simply using her body. If you have felt similarly toward your husband, it may sound nauseating to initiate sex with him on sheer willpower. However, as your relationship grows and deepens, you will find it more natural to give yourself to him and even initiate sexual intimacy.

When you do initiate it from time to time, use imagination to make the bedroom and your appearance as inviting as possible. Perfume, candlelight, gentle words, and a soft touch are just a few of the ways you can add creativity to the occasion.

Another way to make the occasion more fulfilling for you and your husband is for each of you to concentrate on meeting each other's sexual needs. I have found that a selfless, giving attitude contributes most to sexual enjoyment. A man's greatest fulfillment comes when he puts his whole heart into stimulating his wife and bringing her to a climactic experience. At the same time, a woman is most fulfilled when she concentrates on meeting her husband's needs. Selfish sex does nothing but remove the potential for maximum pleasure.

Needless to say, there are dozens, if not hundreds, of books written by authorities on how to make the bedroom experience more fulfilling. But I firmly believe that sex at its best happens when a husband begins to meet his wife's emotional needs on a daily basis. All the techniques and atmosphere in the world can't warm up a neglected wife.

Remain flexible.

Most women would like to have their days scheduled from beginning to end, with no surprises. Schedules can be beneficial when they provide a guide for the day, but they can also become inflexible taskmasters. The day is ruined for some women when one item on their schedule has to be changed. All they can think about when their husbands come home is, "I'm behind on my schedule, and tomorrow will be worse if I don't catch up before bedtime."

If you want your marital relationship to deepen, it is very important that you learn to be flexible. I believe there is nothing as important to you or your family as a good, loving relationship with your husband. Your flexibility can make your husband feel really special and can keep that "spark" in your relationship. When he comes home and sees that you are willing to set aside your schedule for an unrushed conversation, he feels valued and loved.

Occasionally I come home late at night after

meeting with a couple or a group. It really means a lot to me when my wife wakes up and spends a few minutes listening to me unwind as I tell her about my evening. Sure she's making a sacrifice, but it makes me feel important and deepens my affection for her.

Your schedule is important, I realize. However, you need to maintain a balance by being able to set aside your priorities from time to time to pay special attention to your husband and his needs. That's genuine love.

Keep yourself in good physical condition.

Health's most bitter enemies are lack of sleep and an improper diet. When they team up with constant stress, they can leave a woman irritable—not exactly an invitation to her husband's affection.

Believe it or not, one major answer to the problem of fatigue, listlessness, and irritability is regular vigorous exercise, whether it be jogging, bicycling, an exercise class, or working out at a health spa. (Be sure to consult your physician if you have any health problems that might be restrictive to certain types of exercise.)

Increase Your Responsiveness to Your Husband

A man loves a responsive woman. In fact, a man's self-confidence is directly related to the way others respond to him. A man will tie his affection to those who respond to him and remove it from those who don't. There are at least two ways you can increase your responsiveness to your husband.

Maintain an openness and willingness to yield to him.

In suggesting a willingness to yield to your husband, I am not talking about the doormat concept of blind submission. God gave you a mind and feelings that He never intended your husband to trample underfoot. I am talking about the willingness *to be open* to whatever your husband has to say—a willingness to hear him out and yield, if you can do so without violating your own conscience. This type of submission is not a sign of weakness, but a sign of genuine maturity (Ephesians 5:22).

You know your child is growing up when he or she begins to notice and defer to the needs of others. Likewise, adults demonstrate maturity when they are willing to submit for the sake of one another. A man needs to have a submissive attitude toward his wife by considering her feelings and unique personality when making decisions. He needs to be willing at times to yield to her preferences. The more mature we are, the more willing we are to yield to one another.

In marriage, submission is not always simultaneous. Someone has to begin. If it doesn't start with your husband, then why not let it start with you? Perhaps he'll take advantage of your submission at first, but eventually he may take up your mature approach himself.

Carefully consider what your husband says without reacting to him.

Give attentive consideration to what your husband says *without* reacting negatively. Don't just accept the surface meaning of his statements. Ask questions and probe gently until you have a thorough understanding of what he's really trying to say.

Don't play mind reader. Too many wives assume they know their husbands well enough to predict what they are going to say. Some wives even claim to know their husbands' hidden motives. If you're going to assume anything, I hope that you will assume pure motives on your husband's part. If you do, you will be much less resistant and much more responsive to his statements. Don't react to his statements while he's speaking, but consider them and retain anything of value in them.

"You're just being weak," one husband said when his wife asked for an occasional "I love you." Needing reassurance of his love, verbally she had been slapped in the face. Obviously her affectionate feelings were dampened by his comment. Had she only stepped out of the circle of offense and taken time to consider his response, she could have learned a lot— that she needed to share why his expressions of love were important, that he approached the subject from a different reference point, and that he had *not* intended to hurt her.

As you become more responsive to your husband by learning to yield and not react, you will increase his self-confidence and self-worth. As a result, he'll gain a deeper affection for you.

Keep the Imagination in Your Relationship Alive

Most of us are not fond of our daily ruts. We flock to the unusual, the novel, the unexpected in life. It's no wonder that routine marriages break up. There are too many interesting carnivals all around. When a wife can predict her husband's every mood and a husband can predict his wife's, their marriage is in for trouble. As they say, "Variety is the spice of life." So let's put some spice into your marriages.

I jog two to five miles every day, but I never take the same route two days in a row. I don't want my jogging to become monotonous. Variety keeps it interesting. The same holds true for your marriage relationship. Monotony can't set in when you add variety to your dinners, your conversations, your outings, your dates, your sex life, and your appearance.

One of the best ways to keep the imagination alive in your relationship is to be well-informed. Ask your friends how they add creativity to their marriages. Read books and magazines about subjects that would stimulate interesting conversation. My wife contributes so much to the variety of our marriage because she is constantly learning. She not only keeps her mind alert by reading, but she also takes courses on nutrition, gourmet cooking, and other special subjects. It seems she always has something new and interesting to talk about.

Clear Up Your Past Offenses Toward Him

Each time you offend your husband without clearing it up, you drive a wedge in your relationship. Nothing will remove that wedge except your humble request for his forgiveness. Write down at least three or four things you have done recently to offend your husband. Then go to him with a humble attitude and ask his forgiveness. You might even take it a step further and ask him what other areas of your life offend him.

Sally was afraid to try this because her close friend had been blasted when she asked her husband how she could improve as a wife and mother. "But I'm still planning on doing it," Sally said, "because I saw how much it improved my friend's marriage." Sally's friend had finally let her husband's correction sink in and take effect. "She stopped dominating and let him lead out in public," Sally told me, "and it really improved their relationship."

Perhaps the greatest step toward maturity is learning how to admit when we are wrong. When we can humbly seek another's forgiveness, we not only clear the offense but also gain the respect of the offended one. What takes more courage—ignoring your offense or admitting it? The only time I ever sensed a negative reaction when I asked for forgiveness was when I asked with an accusing attitude. When others sensed a lack of genuine sorrow, they often reacted with bitterness or anger. But when they sensed a sincere grief on my part, their respect for me seemed to increase. Not only is God drawn to the humble—so are others (James 4:6).

Remain a Challenge to Your Husband

I've discovered a deep truth in Proverbs: "If a man is hungry, almost anything is sweet; if he is full, even honey is distasteful" (Prov. 27:7, my paraphrase). What a powerful statement of human nature—we all tend to desire what we cannot have and become bored with what we have conquered.

Before you married, you probably were your husband's number one challenge. He got more of a charge out of winning you than anything else in life.

A man is often willing to set aside everything—relationships, projects, vocation—in order to pursue the woman he wants to marry. Unfortunately, soon after the wedding his sense of challenge departs, and he "buries himself" in projects, vocation, and other relationships. "Ah, but if I play hard to get, that'll get my husband's attention," you say. No, that may only frustrate him. But if you maintain a confident independence, showing him that he is not your sole purpose for living, he will feel challenged once again.

Before we were married, I dated my wife sporadically over a period of four years. It seemed Norma was always available. I could call her on a moment's notice and she was always ready to go out with me. She was easy to talk to, and I loved being with her. But I took Norma for granted—perhaps because she was always available when I called her.

Then one day I heard she was dating another guy. For some strange reason my affection for her increased immediately. I thought I was going to lose her. I pursued her vigorously—all the way to the altar. But once we were married, the challenge was over. Boredom began to set in for both of us. Through many of the principles in this book, we overcame the boredom, and to this day Norma remains a challenge to me. I know she is not totally dependent upon me for her happiness. She has a deep relationship with God and looks to Him for her ultimate fulfillment (Ps. 62:1-2; Eph. 3:19-20).

Use Your Natural Attractive Qualities

Several years ago a friend of mine was attending a retreat for college students. He had been married for about four years and was actively involved in counseling college-age young people. On the retreat, a very attractive young girl came to him for counseling. In a moment of emotion, she put her arms around him seeking his comfort. He tells me that to this day, six years later, he can still remember her soft and gentle embrace. He said that in the course of his marriage his wife, who had been so gentle and affectionate when they were dating, had never touched him so softly. But one moment with that young girl had melted him. He said he hasn't seen her since, but he's never forgotten her soft voice and gentle touch.

What has happened to all the lovable characteristics that first attracted your husband to you? Perhaps it was your quiet, gentle voice . . . your gentle spirit . . . your ability to listen . . . your vivacious personality . . . your keen mind . . . your sense of humor . . . whatever qualities made the total person to whom he was initially attracted. Have some of them gotten lost through the years? Do you scream for his attention now? Are you too busy to listen to him? Have you lost your sense of humor?

I realize that your husband's inattentiveness through the years may have drained you of some of these qualities, may have driven you to scream or throw things, may have caused you to ignore him. But if you are to recapture his attention, you must somehow recapture and exhibit those qualities unique to you that first drew him to you. (These same qualities are very likely what might now attract him into the arms of another woman who exhibits them.)

Gently Teach Him by Sharing Your Feelings

Your husband may think he is one of the most affectionate men ever to walk the face of the earth. If he's not, are you willing to teach him how to be? Maybe he assumes going to bed with you is all the affection you need. You and I both know nothing could be further from the truth. When you do share your feelings, wait for the right time and the right circumstances. Present your feelings as clearly and logically as you can. If he reacts negatively to them, wait for another time. But be persistent.

Try not to pressure him, but patiently and gently explain to him how you feel.

Sharing your feelings takes persistence, but it also takes a method that really helps a man to better understand your true feelings. The most effective method I'm aware of is called "feeling word pictures."

These are feeling words related to a man's interests or past experiences.

Here are some examples:

- I feel like I'm a sixty-minute cassette tape and you play me romantically at night like I'm a ten-minute tape.
- I feel like a towel after a full day of washing dirty trucks.
- I feel like a two-hour-old McDonald's hamburger.
- I feel like a worm after catching a big fish.
- I feel like a golf ball after eighteen holes for one important tournament—discarded or ignored.

For Personal Reflection

List at least five ways you are enriching your husband's life and your marriage. Remember 2 Corinthians 9:6.

4

How to Gain
Your Husband's
Appreciation and Praise

> "Her children rise up and bless her; her
> husband also, and he praises her."
> —*Proverbs 31:28*

"Hi, Honey. Just a little note to tell you that I
love you and miss you. Hurry back to me!"

John smiled to himself as he folded the note
and put it back in his wallet. During his ten-
year marriage he has had to travel a lot. He
usually arrives at his hotel discouraged and
lonely. But through the years his wife has
made those times of separation a lot more
pleasant by hiding cards, letters, even cookies
in his suitcase.

"I get a warm feeling whenever I find a
surprise," he says, "because I'm reminded of
her love for me. It really makes me feel better,
though I still miss her."

John kept one of her notes in his billfold during his last business trip. Whenever he was down, he took it out and reread it. The note was a constant reminder of her love and appreciation for him.

John's wife gained his praise and appreciation by freely showing appreciation for him. I have found that everyone has a deep hunger for praise and appreciation. Never in all my years of counseling have I heard a woman complain of too much praise from her husband.

But I have heard the opposite. "My husband is always so critical. If he would only appreciate the things I do." Though many wives may feel there is no hope, I know a husband can learn to praise his wife. I have found two ways a woman can increase her husband's appreciation for her and at the same time stimulate his outward expression of appreciation.

Showing Approval of Your Husband

Men hunger for appreciation from others. They will gladly receive recognition from secretaries, employers, employees, friends, or anyone else willing to give it. A man's need for approval is as strong as your need for security in financial matters and family relationships.

When a man knows his wife approves of him, he enjoys her companionship. He will find himself spontaneously complimenting her in response to the approval she gives.

Instead of demanding appreciation from your husband or shedding tears when he doesn't give it, try the approaches suggested below.

The Direct Approach

One way to show approval is the "direct approach"—expressing esteem for your husband verbally or through letters, love notes, and cards. I'm looking at two cards my wife sent me last month. In the past, I would have opened them and thought, "Isn't that nice?" before tossing them into the nearest trash can. But the more cards and letters I receive from Norma, the more anxious I am to reciprocate her "written praise." Now when I receive a note from her, I usually keep it for several readings. When she sends cards that cite specific qualities she appreciates in me, I feel inspired to think about her praiseworthy qualities and reciprocate with a card.

Though it's true that all men need appreciation, not all men like the same *form* of appreciation. Be careful to avoid forms your husband might find gushy or overly sentimental. You can discern what will encourage your husband and what will embarrass him by trying several ways until a few really hit home.

My heart goes out to one Baylor University coed who hired a fraternity group to sing a Valentine love song to her fiancé. She expected him to react dramatically to the surprise she planned, but he never mentioned it to her.

"Jim, how did you like your Valentine song?" she finally asked.

"Oh, yeah," he said, "I heard it, but I didn't really understand why you did it. It was kind of confusing to me."

His response left her hurt and confused. She honestly wondered if he cared for her at all. This pointed example illustrates something I hope each woman will remember long after this book has been read: men think differently than women.

The exercise below will help you learn how to show approval for your husband. In the left column, list ten admirable areas of his life. In the right column, record how you intend to praise him in that area. You may want to tell him personally or with a special note hidden where he'll be sure to find it. However you choose to do it, let it be your way of saying,

"Honey, I really approve of what you've done and who you are." Remember, we can value people even if they irritate us.

Things You Approve of About Your Husband	Direct and Creative Ways to Show Your Approval
1. _____	_____
2. _____	_____
3. _____	_____
4. _____	_____
5. _____	_____
6. _____	_____
7. _____	_____
8. _____	_____
9. _____	_____
10. _____	_____

The Indirect Approach

The "indirect" approach is another way to show approval of your husband. Husbands and wives were using this approach long before the flood of marriage books hit the market.

Norma's mother had this approach down pat years ago. Through good grooming and an encouraging five o'clock greeting, she showed "indirect" approval of her husband. Every day she prepared for his homecoming by bathing and putting on fresh clothing. Norma says she can't remember a single time when her mother greeted her father with problems or complaints. Instead, she let him relax and made him feel important by the extra time and effort she spent to make one part of his day happy.

Norma's mom was a good teacher. I have never come home to the wife portrayed in cartoons—dressed in a sagging, torn housecoat and curlers as permanent as light fixtures. Norma always looks good and smells good.

I could list thousands of indirect ways to show approval for your husband. Norma knows plenty of them. Just to name a few: she welcomes my suggestions about her wardrobe; she introduces me to new friends with a tone of voice that reflects admiration for me; and she constantly tells our children how much she appreciates me.

I remember the time when I came home from work dead on my feet, too tired to protest when my daughter climbed into my lap with sticky fingers. "Daddy, Mommy says you work real hard to take good care of us." A warm sensation spread over me, and suddenly I didn't feel so tired. (Chances are, your children will let your husband know what's being said "behind his back." I hope for his sake that it's good.)

Praise your husband to his male friends and their wives. Just think what good gossip you'll spread when you say positive things about your spouse. Quite a switch from the usual complaints!

At this point, make a long list of the indirect ways you can show approval for your husband. Pick two or three of the best ones and be sure to apply them during the next week.

Three Ways to Alienate Your Husband

Wives often alienate their husbands by *unknowingly expressing disapproval of them.* Here's how one woman's disapproval drove a wedge between her husband and her.

Joan always greeted Frank at the door with pushy advice about this problem or that decision. He began to dread his homecoming each day because he envisioned Joan as a stalking lion, ready to pounce on him.

One evening, before he could even put down his briefcase, Joan pounced. "I heard what you said to the Jacksons at the company party. I thought about it all day." Frank's stomach knotted in a hot wad as he blocked out her words. But her shrill voice pierced his defense. "Frank! Frank! You never listen to me. I want you to call the Jacksons right now and invite them to dinner next week. We have to be friends with them if you ever want to get anywhere in the company."

I can't believe she thinks I'm so dumb, Frank thought. *Why does she keep pushing me?*

A man often interprets his wife's bossiness as a lack of approval. *She must not think I'm too capable, judging from all the advice she gives me.*

In defense of many wives, I recognize that the passive nature of the typical husband forces a wife to "take over." I hear how very frustrating it is for you. My encouragement is that a natural response doesn't always gain the result you desire. One paraphrase of Ephesians 5:22 is, "Let your husband take care of your needs just as you allow the Lord to love you."

Another way wives show disapproval for their husbands is by *discrediting their feelings or desires.* As a highly skilled art critic, one wife decides to quietly dispose of his pitiful Rembrandt reproduction. As an expert seamstress, another wife criticizes that "custom-made" suit he got on sale. Or, on a more realistic plane, the veteran gardener ignores her husband's desire to plant a pine tree on the front lawn and opts for a maple instead.

If you will listen closely, you can hear your husband expressing his desires every hour. Right now he may be mumbling behind his newspaper about chicken spaghetti with sour sauce and cherries on top like his mother used to make. Pick up on his subtle statement and make it for him. If you don't, he'll wonder whether he's worth anything to you. Resentment may spring up alongside his doubt, and soon he'll make unconscious efforts to eliminate things that please you. "I know what you want, but I don't want to do it" becomes the sad response of many husbands.

You may have to run on sheer willpower to respond to your husband's desires at first. But remember, good feelings usually follow loving actions. Who knows? You may even learn to like his mother's chicken spaghetti concoction.

As proof of your good intentions, write down at least ten things you know are important to your husband. Schedule one or two a week for him. The best way to obtain a completely accurate list is to ask him. "Honey, I'd like to sit down and find out what things in life are really important to you." His response may provide a list that will outlast your retirement years.

The third and most common way wives show disapproval of their husbands is by *contradicting them*. Have you ever sympathised with a husband who could hardly get a word out of his mouth before his wife jumped in with both feet to correct him? "No, that's not the way it was. It was like this. . . ."

Contradiction is hardly an invitation to most husbands. No one wants to live with a know-it-all.

When Frank and Mary came to my office for marital counseling, she was by far the more "motivated" of the two. She answered not only the questions addressed to her but also those addressed to her husband.

"Now, Frank," I asked, "how do you see the situation?"

Before Frank could utter a sound, Mary would interrupt and say, "He'll say something about me, but it won't be true. He exaggerates."

I rarely become irritated in counseling sessions, but this time I began to boil within.

I asked, "Frank, what do you think the

problem is?" and Mary said, "I think it's that he never spends any time with me."

Time after time, Mary answered Frank's questions. Even when he did speak up for himself, Mary had a countercharge that put him to shame. Several perplexing questions came to mind. Was the woman deaf? Had I misunderstood them when they introduced themselves—was her name Frank and his Mary?

This kind of problem usually indicates a very passive, noncommunicative husband. She's had to answer for him if any type of communication was to occur between them. However, after a while he interprets this method as a put-down.

I suggest that with this type of person you: (1) direct questions to him in a loving, accepting manner to draw him out; (2) wait for him to express himself; (3) praise him for each genuine idea he expresses.

List the ways you have contradicted your husband lately and make a silent promise to forsake them in the future. Each time you are tempted to contradict him in front of someone, step into his shoes and imagine the embarrassment he will feel.

Gently Teach Your Husband
About Your Need for His Approval

Judy loved teaching because her principal commended her regularly for her skills and methods. Rarely did a day pass without a gentle, encouraging word from him. It seemed the more he praised her work, the better she became.

Imagine the effect constant praise would have on your attitude as a wife. You would work harder each day to *be* the mate your husband talked about. You would also be absolutely free to praise him once you knew your work was appreciated. Don't be embarrassed to request his praise. There's nothing wrong with the boost you receive from sincere praise.

Norma once overheard a grocery store clerk explain how much she loved her job because the friendliness of the customers made her feel accepted and needed. "And my boss and the other clerks tell me I do a good job, too," she said. "I'd rather be here where somebody appreciates me than at home with that husband of mine. Even if I fix a ten-course meal, he doesn't notice. But just let me be late with dinner once! Then I hear about it."

This woman needed to admit her need for his approval. If a woman can't admit her need for praise, then her marriage will become stale and superficial. Her feelings of love and responsiveness will dry up, and she will start building walls to keep her husband at a distance. A woman will never completely feel like her husband's helper and completer until she *hears* how she is helping and completing (Genesis 2:18).

Be specific with your husband about when you need his praise. Try something like, "I know you want a happy marriage. Dear, would you like to know what you can do to make me a very happy wife? It won't cost you a thing. No energy—just a little creativity."

"What?"

"You can show your approval of me by praising me for who I am and what I do. For instance, I especially need your praise when I fix a special meal for you or go out of my way to do something extra. I just need to know how you liked it. I need it, and it's okay to need it."

Perhaps you can best explain your need for appreciation by relating it to one of your husband's personal experiences. When one husband asked his wife why she wouldn't take a vacation with him, she responded, "Would you want to take a vacation with your old boss?" (He had just quit his job due to harsh criticism from his boss.)

His wife gently explained, "When you criticize me, I feel like you do when your boss criticizes you. I feel defeated when you ignore the good things about my meals and point out what I forgot, like—'The salt isn't on the table,' or 'You didn't buy the right kind of butter.' Even though we both have jobs, I feel you expect me to fix dinner while you watch television. I feel less than a person."

Dale broke down and cried. Within six months, he was a completely different person. Having conquered the temptation to complain, he is now free to meet his wife's need for approval and praise.

Light Up When He Praises You

The last way to teach your husband about your need for approval is to "light up" whenever he praises you. Reward him with enthusiasm and excitement, making him subconsciously desirous of praising you more often.

As human beings, we all need and respond to praise. There is nothing shameful about longing for an occasional "pat on the back." So demonstrate your legitimate need by responding to your husband's praise with a cheerful face and bright expressions. He will be sure to remember it next time you need approval.

For Personal Reflection

Memorize Ephesians 4:29. List the words you can use to build up (edify) your husband. Then list the words that tear him down so you can avoid these. What comes out of our mouths should encourage and lift another (Ephesians 4:29).

Other Books by Gary Smalley

Decide to Love (Leader's Resource Kit)
Decide to Love (Student's Manual)
For Better or For Best
If Only He Knew
The Joy of Committed Love